Nita Mehta's

Vegetarian
CURRIES

Nita Mehta

B.Sc. (Home Science), M.Sc. (Food and Nutrition), Gold Medalist

Tanya Mehta

SNAB
Excellence in Books

Nita Mehta's
Vegetarian
CURRIES

Snab Publishers Pvt Ltd

Corporate Office
3A/3, Asaf Ali Road, New Delhi 110 002
Phone: +91 11 2325 2948, 2325 0091
Telefax: +91 11 2325 0091
E-mail: nitamehta@nitamehta.com
Website: www.nitamehta.com

ISBN 978-81-7869-041-4

5th Print 2011

Printed in India by Nutech Photolithographers

Cover desined by: **flyingtrees**

Distributed by :
NITA MEHTA BOOKS
3A/3, Asaf Ali Road, New Delhi - 02

Distribution Centre :
D16/1, Okhla Industrial Area, Phase-I,
New Delhi - 110020
Tel.: 26813199, 26813200
E-mail: nitamehta.mehta@gmail.com

Editorial and Marketing office
E-159, Greater Kailash II, New Delhi 110 048

Food Styling and Photography by Snab
Typesetting by National Information Technology Academy
3A/3, Asaf Ali Road, New Delhi 110 002

Recipe Development & Testing:
Nita Mehta Foods - R & D Centre
3A/3, Asaf Ali Road, New Delhi - 110002
E-143, Amar Colony, Lajpat Nagar-IV, New Delhi - 110024

Price: Rs. 89/-

Introduction

*T*o most, curry simply means vegetables with gravy, along with a combination of spices. One always thinks a curry to be something oily, rich and hot. We have tried our best to change this concept by reducing oil and chillies and adding flavourful spices. The curries are flavoured with exotic spices like nutmeg (*jaiphal*), mace (*javetri*), saffron (*kesar*), black cardamoms (*moti illaichi*), green cardamoms (*chhoti illaichi*), fennel seeds (*saunf*), cinnamon (*dalchini*) etc.

The curries are grouped on the basis of their colour – Red, Yellow, Green, White and Brown. Although a green curry will not always be a perfect green, but it will certainly have a hint of green in it. Similarly, a white curry will not be pure white as it will take some colour from the spices added to it.

This division is done to make your table spread look attractive when you serve a meal.

Nita Mehta

ABOUT THE RECIPES

WHAT'S IN A CUP?

INDIAN CUP
1 teacup = 200 ml liquid
AMERICAN CUP
1 cup = 240 ml liquid (8 oz.)
The recipes in this book were tested with the Indian teacup which holds 200 ml liquid.

Contents

White Curries 31

Annari Makai 32
Vegetable Korma 34
Methi Malai Matar 36

Makhmali Babycorns 38
Mirchi Ka Saalan 41
Punjabi Matar Tamatar in Gravy 43

Yellow Curries 45

Capsicums in Sesame Curry 46
Kandhari Bharwaan Khumb 48
Brinjals in Coconut Gravy 51
Rajasthani Arbi 53

Achaari Paneer 55
Paneer Makai Curry 58
Shahi Kaju Aloo 60
Punjabi Kadhi 62

Green Curries 64

Green Mushroom Curry 65
Broccoli Curry 67

Paalak Chaman 69
Matar Dhania Wale 71

Paneer in Pista Gravy   73
Chutney Wale Aloo   76

Malai Kofte in Paalak   78
Hari Dal   80

Brown Curries   81

Paneer in Tamarind Coconut
Curry   82
Vegetable Sticks in Curry   84
Mughlai Dum Aloo   88

Nawabi Guchhi   90
Paneer Chettinad   92
Parval ka Dum   94
Dal Makhani   96

Indian Rice & Breads
Paranthas, Nans & Rotis   99

Onion & Mint Rice   100
Lachha Parantha   101

Tandoori Roti   102

Red Curries

Rajasthani Bharwaan Lauki

Roundels of bottle gourd stuffed with paneer. Must give it a try.

Serves 4-6   *Picture on page 57*

500 gm lauki (bottle gourd) - medium thickness

FILLING

200 gm paneer - crumbled (mash roughly)
1 tsp finely chopped ginger
1 green chilli - finely chopped
2 tbsp chopped green coriander
8-10 kaju (cashewnuts) - chopped
8-10 kishmish (raisins) - soaked in warm water for 10 minutes
¾ tsp salt or to taste

MASALA

2 tbsp oil or ghee
2 laung (cloves)
2 tej patta (bay leaves)

Contd...

seeds of 2 chhoti illaichi (green cardamoms)
1" stick dalchini (cinnamon)

TOMATO PASTE (Grind Together to a paste)
3 tomatoes
1 green chilli
½" piece ginger
½ tsp red chilli powder
1 tsp dhania powder
¼ tsp haldi, ¾ tsp salt
½ tsp jeera (cumin seeds)
¼ tsp sugar

1. Peel lauki. Cut vertically into two pieces from the centre to get 2 smaller pieces.
2. Boil in salted water with 1 tsp lemon juice, covered, for about 10 minutes, till done. Remove from water and cool.
3. Scoop seeds from both the pieces of the lauki and make them hollow.
4. Mix paneer, ginger, green chilli, coriander, cashewnuts, kishmish and salt.
5. Stuff it into the boiled lauki pieces. Keep aside.

6. For masala, heat ghee. Add laung, illaichi, dalchini & tej patta. Stir for a minute.
7. Add the above tomato paste. Stir for 3-4 minutes till thick and oil separates.
8. Add 1½ cups water. Boil. Simmer for 4-5 minutes till oil separates. Keep aside.
9. At serving time, saute lauki in a flat kadhai or a non stick pan in 1-2 tbsp oil, turning sides carefully to brown from all sides. Cover for a while so that the filling also gets heated. Remove from pan.
10. Cut the lauki into ¾" thick round pieces. Transfer to a serving dish and pour the hot tomato gravy on top. Serve.

Mirch~Makai Ka Salan

Thick green chillies and corn in a tamarind based Hyderabadi gravy.
If thick green chillies are not available, use the regular ones.

Serves 5-6

12 pieces (150 gm) baby corns - cut lengthwise into 2 pieces
12 big green chillies - slit and deseeded
1 large onion - ground to a paste
½ cup tomato puree or 3 tomatoes - pureed
½" piece ginger - grated
¼ tsp of haldi (turmeric powder)
1 tsp dhania powder, ½ tsp garam masala
1¼ tsp salt, or to taste, ½ tsp pepper, or to taste
1 cups milk
½ cup cream (optional)

PASTE
2 tbsp cashews (kaju) - soaked in warm water and ground to a paste

1. Heat 4 tbsp oil. Add green chillies and fry for 3-4 minutes till they turn slightly whitish. Remove from oil and keep aside.
2. Add baby corns and fry for 3-4 minutes till brown specs appear. Remove from oil and keep aside.
3. Heat the remaining oil. Add onion, fry till light brown.
4. Add haldi, dhania and garam masala. Stir for a minute.
5. Add tomato puree. Cook for 5 minutes on low heat till dry and oil separates.
6. Add cashew paste. Mix.
7. Add 1 cup water and boil. Add salt and pepper to taste. Add fried baby corns. Simmer on low flame for 10 minutes.
8. Add ginger. Remove from fire and keep aside till serving time.
9. At serving time, add milk gradually, stirring well, to the curry. Mix well and put on low heat, stirring continuously till it just boils. Add green chillies and cream. Remove from heat immediately and serve.

Note : Choose green chillies which are thick, big and light green, as the small, dark green ones are hotter. Remember, to deseed them. After deseeding them, tap them gently to remove all the seeds.

Makhani Babycorn

Baby corns with capsicums in a simple yet delicious gravy.

Serves 5-6

10-12 pieces (150 gm) baby corns - cut lengthwise into 2 long pieces
2 capsicums - cut into 1" square pieces
1 large onion - ground to a paste
4 tomatoes - ground to a puree
1" piece ginger - grated
¼ tsp haldi
1 tsp dhania powder (ground coriander)
½ tsp garam masala
1¼ tsp salt, or to taste, ½ tsp red chilli powder
1 cup milk, see note
½ cup cream (optional)

PASTE
2 tbsp cashews (kaju) - soaked in warm water and ground to a paste

1. Heat 4 tbsp oil. Add capsicums and fry for a minute till crisp. Remove from oil and keep aside.
2. Add baby corns and fry for 3-4 minutes till brown specs appear. Remove from oil and keep aside.
3. Heat the remaining oil. Add onion paste, fry till light brown.
4. Add haldi, dhania powder and garam masala. Stir for a minute.
5. Add fresh pureed tomatoes. Cook for 5 minutes on low heat till dry and oil separates.
6. Add cashew paste. Mix.
7. Add 1 cup of water and boil. Add red chilli powder and salt to taste. Add fried baby corns. Simmer on low flame for 10 minutes till thick.
8. Add grated ginger. Remove from fire and keep aside till serving time.
9. At serving time, add milk to the thick masala to get a gravy. Mix well. Keep on low heat, stirring continuously till it comes to a boil.
10. Add fried capsicums and cream. Remove from heat and serve immediately.

Note: The milk should never be added to the hot tomato gravy. Let it cool down before adding the milk. Never boil the gravy too much after the milk has been added. It might curdle if done so.

Stuffed Tomatoes in Gravy

Picture on facing page   *Serves 4*

6 small firm tomatoes, 2-3 tbsp oil

FILLING

150 gms (1½ cups) paneer - grated
4 cashews (kaju) - crushed
1 tsp raisins (kishmish) - soak in warm water for 15 minutes & drained
2-3 tbsp chopped coriander, 2 green chillies
1 tsp chaat masala, ½ tsp salt or to taste, ½ tsp garam masala
½ tsp red chilli powder

GRAVY

2 big onions, 1" piece ginger
½ cup curd
½ tsp haldi, 1 tsp dhania powder
½ tsp chilli powder, ¾ tsp salt, ½ tsp garam masala
2 tbsp tomato ketchup
3 tbsp chopped fresh dhania (coriander)

1. Slice a small piece from the top of each tomato. Scoop out carefully, (to make place for stuffing the filling). Keep the scooped tomato pulp aside for the gravy.
2. Rub some salt on the inside of tomatoes and keep them upside down for 10 minutes.
3. Grate paneer. Add all other ingredients of the filling & mix gently. Do not mash.
4. Heat 2-3 tbsp oil in a pan and gently fry the scooped tomatoes in it. Cook on low flame for 3-4 minutes, changing sides till tomatoes become a little soft. Let them get charred (blackened) at some places. Remove from oil. Alternately, rub a little oil over the tomatoes and grill in a hot oven for 8-10 minutes. Do not let them be in the oven for a longer period, otherwise they will turn limp. Keep aside. Let it cool.
5. Fill the scooped and fried tomatoes with the filling. Press well. Keep the left over filling (2 tbsp) aside for the gravy.
6. To prepare the gravy, grind onions, ginger and the scooped out portion of the tomatoes, together in a blender.
7. Heat 3-4 tbsp oil. Add the onion-tomato paste and cook till dry. Cook further for 3-4 minutes till oil separates.
8. Reduce heat. Beat curd lightly with a fork & add gradually to the above masala.

9. Cook stirring continuously on low flame till the masala turns dry & oil separates.
10. Add haldi, dhania powder, chilli powder, salt and garam masala. Cook for 1 minute.
11. Add 1½ cups hot water and tomato ketchup to get a thick gravy. Boil. Simmer on low flame for 7- 8 minutes, till oil separates.
12. Add left over paneer of the filling (2 tbsp) and coriander. Mix well. Keep aside.
13. To serve, put some hot gravy in a serving dish. Heat stuffed tomatoes in an oven and arrange on the hot gravy. Sprinkle some hot gravy on the top also. If you have a microwave, then arrange in a serving dish and heat together.

Cheesy Broccoli Koftas

Serves 4-6

1 medium broccoli - grated finely along with tender stalks (2 cups grated)
1 potatoes - boiled and grated
2 tbsp roasted peanuts (moongphali) - crushed coarsely
¼ tsp coarsely crushed saboot kali mirch (peppercorns)
½ tsp salt, ¼ tsp garam masala, ¼ tsp amchoor
1½ tbsp cornflour, a pinch of baking powder
1 cheese cube (20 gm) - cut into 10 pieces, ½ tbsp butter

GRAVY
3 tbsp oil
5 tomatoes - pureed or 1 cup ready made tomato puree
1 tsp jeera (cumin seeds)
1" piece ginger - grated, 1 tsp ginger paste, 4 tbsp chopped coriander
4 tbsp chopped coriander
1¼ tsp salt, ¾ tsp garam masala, 1½ tsp dhania powder, ½ tsp red chilli powder
1 cup water, 1 cup milk
¼-½ cup cream or fresh malai

1. Grate the broccoli florets and the tender stems very finely.
2. Heat butter in a pan. Add chopped broccoli. Add ¼ tsp salt. Stir on medium heat for 3-4 minutes on low heat. Remove from heat.
3. Grate the potato well. Add peanuts, salt, crushed peppercorns, garam masala, amchoor, cornflour, baking powder and cooked broccoli to the potato.
4. Make balls of the potato-broccoli mixture.
5. Flatten a ball and put a small piece of cheese in it. Make a ball again.
6. Deep fry 2-3 balls at a time till golden. Drain on absorbent paper.
7. To prepare the gravy, heat oil. Add jeera. Let it turn golden.
8. When golden, add ginger shreds and ginger paste. Stir for a few seconds.
9. Add tomato puree. Add salt, garam masala, dhania powder and red chilli. Cook for 5-8 minutes, till puree turns dry and oil separates. Add chopped coriander, mix. Add enough water to get a thick gravy. Boil. Cook on low heat for 4-5 minutes. Remove from fire. Let it cool down.
10. To serve, add enough milk to the cold gravy stirring continuously. Add koftas. Keep on low heat and stir continuously till just about to boil. Add cream and remove from fire after 2-3 seconds. Serve.

Dakshini Paneer Makhani

Serves 4

250 gm paneer - cut into 1" cubes
5 large (500 gm) tomatoes - each cut into 4 pieces
2 tbsp desi ghee or butter and 2 tbsp oil, ½ tsp jeera (cumin seeds)
4-5 flakes garlic & 1" piece ginger - ground to a paste
1 tbsp kasoori methi (dried fenugreek leaves), 1 tsp tomato ketchup
2 tsp dhania powder, ½ tsp garam masala
1 tsp salt, or to taste, ½ tsp red chilli powder, preferably degi mirch
½ cup water, ½-1 cup milk, approx., ½ cup cream (optional)

KAJU PASTE

3 tbsp kaju - soaked in ¼ cup warm water for 15 minutes & ground to a paste

TADKA

1 tbsp oil, ½ tsp rai, 3-4 tbsp curry leaves, a pinch of red chilli powder

1. Boil tomatoes in ½ cup water. Simmer for 4-5 minutes on low heat till tomatoes turn soft. Remove from fire and cool. Grind the tomatoes along with the water to a smooth puree.

2. Heat oil and ghee or butter in a kadhai. Reduce heat. Add jeera. When it turns golden, add ginger-garlic paste.
3. When paste starts to change colour add the above tomato puree and cook till absolutely dry.
4. Add kasoori methi and tomato ketchup.
5. Add masalas - dhania powder, garam masala, salt and red chilli powder. Mix well for a few seconds. Cook till oil separates.
6. Add finely ground kaju paste. Mix well for 2 minutes.
7. Add water. Boil. Simmer on low heat for 4-5 minutes. Reduce heat.
8. Add the paneer cubes. Keep aside to cool for about 5 minutes.
9. Add enough milk to cold masala to get a thick curry, mix gently. (Remember to add milk only to cold masala, to prevent it from curdling)
10. Heat on low heat, stirring continuously till just about to boil.
11. Add cream, keeping the heat very low and stirring continuously. Remove from fire immediately and transfer to a serving dish.
12. For tadka, heat oil. Add rai. After 30 seconds add curry leaves. Stir.
13. Remove from fire. Add chilli powder and pour over hot gravy in dish.

Akbari Mushrooms

If mushrooms are not available, any vegetable could be used instead.

Serves 8

200 gm mushrooms
juice of ½ lemon, 1 tsp salt, 1 tbsp butter, ¼ tsp pepper
2 tbsp almonds (badaam) - soaked for 10 minutes in hot water, peeled and ground
to a paste with ¼ cup water
1 cup milk, 10-12 cashews (kaju), 1 tbsp oil

MASALA

2 small onions, 4 tomatoes, 1" ginger, 1 green chilli - grind to a paste together
½ tsp shah jeera (royal black cumin)
1 tsp dhania (coriander) powder, ½ tsp amchoor, 1½ tsp salt, 4 tbsp oil
½ tsp red chilli powder, 1 tsp garam masala, 1 tsp tandoori masala
2-3 chhoti illaichi (green cardamom) - seeds crushed
50 -100 gms paneer - grated (½-1 cup), 3 tbsp chopped coriander

BAGHAR OR TEMPERING

1 tbsp oil, ½ tsp shah jeera (black cumin), 1 tsp finely chopped ginger
5-6 almonds (badaam) - cut into thin long pieces, ¼ tsp red chilli powder

1. Wash mushrooms. Keep mushrooms whole and just trim the stalks, cutting only the end tip of the stem.
2. Boil 4 cups water with 1 tsp salt and lime juice. Add mushrooms. Boil for 2 minutes. Drain, refresh in cold water. Wipe dry
3. Heat 1 tbsp oil in a pan. Add kaju and stir till golden. Remove.
4. Heat 1 tbsp butter and saute mushrooms on high heat till dry. Sprinkle pepper and mix. Remove from fire.
5. Heat oil. Add shah jeera. After a minute, add onion-tomato paste and cook till dry and oil separates. Reduce flame. Add red chilli powder, dhania, amchoor, salt and garam masala. Cook for 1 minute.
6. Add almond paste. Stir to mix well.
7. Keeping the flame low, add milk, stirring continuously. Stir for 2-3 minutes.
8. Add enough (2-3 cups approx.) water to get a thin gravy. Boil.
9. Add mushrooms and simmer for 2-3 minutes till slightly thick. Add tandoori masala, chhoti illaichi, paneer and coriander.
10. Transfer to a serving dish. Heat oil. Add jeera and ginger. After a few seconds, add almonds and stir. Add red chilli powder, remove from fire and pour the oil on the hot gravy in the dish. Serve immediately.

Multi Storeyed Paneer

Picture on facing page   *Serves 8*

700-800 gm paneer - cut into a long, thick slab (7" long and 2" thick, approx.)
salt, red chilli powder, haldi and chat masala to sprinkle
2 tbsp oil, 2-3 tbsp grated cheese

FILLING (MIX TOGETHER)
½ cup grated carrot (½ carrot), ¼ cup chopped coriander
4-5 tbsp grated mozzarella or pizza cheese
¼ tsp salt and ¼ tsp freshly ground pepper, ½ tsp oregano, or to taste

TOMATO SAUCE
5 tomatoes - chopped roughly & boiled with ½ cup water
6 tbsp ready made tomato puree, 2 tbsp oil, 1 tsp crushed garlic (6-8 flakes)
½ tsp black pepper, ½ tsp salt and ¼ tsp pepper, or to taste, 3 tbsp cream

GARNISH
a few capsicum strips and tomato pieces, some pepper, 1 tbsp grated cheese

1. To prepare the sauce, boil chopped tomatoes in ½ cup water. Keep on low heat for 4-5 minutes till soft. Remove from fire. Mash and strain.

Discard the skin. Keep fresh tomato puree aside.

2. Heat oil. Reduce heat. Add garlic and stir till it just starts to change colour. Do not make it brown.

3. Add 6 tbsp ready-made tomato puree. Cook till oil separates.

4. Add the prepared fresh tomato puree and give one boil. Simmer on low heat for 5-6 minutes. Remove from fire. Cool to room temperature.

5. Mix in cream. Add salt and pepper to taste and keep the sauce aside.

6. Cut paneer into 3 equal pieces lengthwise, getting big pieces of about ½" thick slices. Do not make them too thick. Sprinkle salt, chilli powder, haldi and chat masala on both sides of each slice of paneer. Saute in 2 tbsp oil in a pan, changing sides carefully, till golden on both sides.

7. In a shallow rectangular serving dish, put ¼ of the prepared tomato sauce. Place a paneer slab on the sauce.

8. Spread ½ of carrot filling on it. Press another piece of paneer on it.

9. Again put the filling on it. Cover with the last piece of paneer. Press.

10. Pour sauce all over paneer to cover top and sides completely. Grate cheese on top. Garnish with tomatoes and capsicum. Sprinkle pepper.

11. Microwave, loosely covered with cling film, on high for 2 minutes. If using an oven, cover with foil and heat for10 minutes at 180°C till hot.

White Curries

Annari Makai

Yellow baby corns with red pomegranates in a white gravy look beautiful.
If baby corns are not available, regular corn on the cob can be used instead.

Serves 6

200 gm baby corns or 2 small tender bhutte (corn on the cobs)
1 tbsp butter, ¼ tsp pepper
1 cup milk
½ cup red kandhari anaar ke daane (fresh red pomegranate)

PASTE

3 onions, 1½" piece ginger, 2 dry red chillies - grind together to a paste

OTHER INGREDIENTS FOR GRAVY

4 tbsp kaju (cashewnuts) - powdered
4-5 chhoti illaichi (green cardamoms)
½ tsp garam masala, ¾ tsp red chilli powder, 1½ tsp salt, or to taste
1 cup milk mixed with 2 cups water
2 tbsp cream, optional

1. Choose small bhuttas or thin tender bhuttas. Keep baby corns whole or cut each bhutta into 4 small pieces. If thick, slit each piece into two.
2. Put all pieces of baby corns and ½ cup milk in a pan. Give one boil and keep on low heat for 2 minutes. If using bhuttas, use a pressure cooker to cook them. Pressure cook bhutta pieces with 1 cup milk to give one whistle. Then keep on low flame for 5 minutes. Remove from fire.
3. Heat 1 tbsp butter & saute corns on high heat for 2-3 minutes. Sprinkle ¼ tsp pepper and mix. Remove from fire.
4. For gravy, grind onions, ginger and dry, red chillies to a fine paste.
5. Heat 4 tbsp oil in a heavy bottomed kadhai and add chhoti illaichi. Wait for ½ minute.
6. Add onion paste. Cook on low flame for about 7-8 minutes, till onions turn light golden. Do not let onions turn brown – cook on low heat.
7. Add masalas - garam masala, red chilli powder and salt.
8. Add kaju powder. Cook for ½ minute.
9. Add milk mixed with water. Boil. Simmer on low flame for 5 minutes.
10. Add corn and simmer on low flame for 3 minutes.
11. At serving time, add anaar ke daane & give one quick boil. Serve immediately, sprinkled with cream and with some more anaar ke daane.

Vegetable Korma

Curd, coconut and cashews form the base of a good korma.
A little cream (¼ cup) can be added at the time of serving.

Picture on page 103   *Serves 4*

½ cup shelled peas
2 small carrots - cut into round slices
6 french beans - cut into ½" diagonal pieces
6-8 small florets (1" pieces) of cauliflower - fried till golden and cooked
1-2 small slices of tinned pineapple - cut into 1" pieces, optional (see note)
2 onions - chopped finely
½ tsp garam masala, 1½ - 2 tsp salt, or to taste
¼ cup cream, optional, some chopped coriander

GRIND TOGETHER TO A PASTE

3 tbsp cashews (kaju) - soaked in warm water for 10 minutes and drained
¾ cup curd, 2 tbsp grated coconut (fresh or desiccated)
½" piece ginger, 3-4 flakes garlic, 2 tsp dhania saboot (coriander seeds)
seeds of 2-3 chhoti illaichi (green cardamom)

1. Soak kaju. Drain. Grind them with coconut, ginger, garlic, saboot dhania and chhoti illaichi together to a paste alongwith curd.
2. Heat 4 tbsp oil. Add onions. Cook till onions turn golden brown.
3. Add the kaju- curd paste. Cook on low heat for 3-4 minutes.
4. Add salt and garam masala. Stir for a few seconds.
5. Add french beans, peas and carrots. Stir for 2 minutes.
6. Add 1½ cup water or enough to get a thick gravy. Boil. Simmer covered for 8-10 minutes till the vegetables get done.
7. Add cauliflower and pineapple. Boil for 1 minute. Add cream.
8. Serve sprinkled with chopped coriander.

Note: If you want to use fresh pineapple, it should be peeled, cut into pieces and cooked in water for about 5 minutes before adding to the gravy.

If using tinned pineapple, the left over tinned pineapple can be stored in a steel or plastic box in the freezer compartment of the refrigerator without getting spoilt for 2 months or more.

Methi Malai Matar

Shreds of dry fenugreek leaves (kasoori methi) make this white curry really appetizing.

Serves 4

200 gms paneer (cottage cheese) - cut into small, ½" cubes
½ cup boiled or frozen peas
½ stick dalchini (cinnamon)
2 moti illaichi (cardamoms)
3-4 laung (cloves)
1 tbsp cashewnuts (kaju)
2 tbsp oil
1 large onion - ground to a paste
¼ tsp white pepper powder
½ cup (75 gms) malai (cream) - beat with ½ cup milk till smooth
4 tbsp kasoori methi (dry fenugreek leaves)
salt to taste
a pinch of sugar
½ - ¾ cup milk (approx.)

1. Crush together dalchini, laung and seeds of moti illaichi on a chakla-belan. Keep the masala aside.
2. Grind cashewnuts separately in a small spice grinder to a fine powder.
3. Heat oil. Add ground onion and cook on low heat till oil separates. Do not let the onion turn brown.
4. Add the crushed masala and pepper powder. Cook for a few seconds.
5. Add kasoori methi and malai, cook on low heat for 2-3 minutes till malai dries up slightly.
6. Add boiled peas and paneer.
7. Add powdered cashewnuts and cook for a few seconds.
8. Add enough milk (½ cup-¾ cup) to get a thick gravy.
9. Add salt and sugar to taste.
10. Serve garnished with some cashewnut bits, roasted on a tawa till golden.

Makhmali Babycorns

Picture on facing page   Serves 3-4

10 baby corns - cut into 2 pieces vertically to get 2 smaller pieces
1 tsp sarson (mustard seeds)
1 tsp dhuli urad dal, 1 tsp channe ki dal
¼ tsp jeera (cumin seeds), ½ tsp saboot dhania (coriander seeds)
a pinch of hing (asafoetida)
1 tsp green chilli - chopped
1 onion - sliced
2 cups of yogurt - hang in a muslin cloth for 15 minutes
½ tsp white pepper powder
½ tsp garam masala, ½ tsp coriander powder
½ tsp salt or to taste
pinch of jaiphal powder (nutmeg)
½" piece dalchini - powdered (cinnamon powder)
2 tbsp very finely chopped coriander leaves
2 tbsp cream (optional)

Capsicums in Sesame Curry: Recipe on page 46, Makhmali Babycorns ➤

1. Boil 2 cups water with ½ tsp salt and a pinch of haldi. Add the babycorns and boil for 2-3 minutes. Drain. Refresh in cold water and keep aside.
2. Collect together - sarson, dhuli urad dal, channe ki dal, jeera & saboot dhania.
3. Heat 2 tbsp oil. Add the collected ingredients. Fry for few a minute till dals turn golden yellow.
4. Add hing and green chillies. Stir.
5. Add sliced onions and fry till light golden (do not make them brown). Remove from fire. Let it cool down.
6. After the onion masala cools down, add hung curd, white pepper powder, garam masala, coriander powder and salt. Return to fire. Cook, stirring till oil separates.
7. Add jaiphal, dalchini powder and baby corns. Bhuno for 2 minutes.
8. Add 1 cups water and coriander. Cook on slow fire for 5-6 minutes.
9. Add cream. Cook for a minute, stirring on low heat. Remove from fire. Serve hot.

Mirchi Ka Salan

Mirchi ka Saalan is whole green chillies in a masala gravy. A popular Hyderabadi dish!

Serves 4-5   *Picture on cover*

250 gm large green chillies - make a slit on one side
4 medium onions - cut each into 4-6 pieces
2 small lemon size balls of tamarind - soak in 1 cup warm water for 15 minutes
1½ tbsp chopped ginger
2 tbsp chopped garlic
1 tbsp coriander seeds (*sabut dhania*), 1 tsp cumin seeds (*jeera*)
.3 tbsp sesame seeds, ¼ cup roasted peanuts
1½ tsp poppy seeds, 2" piece kopra - thickly sliced (dry nariyal)
¼ tsp fenugreek seeds, ¼ tsp turmeric powder
1 tsp red chilli powder, 1 tsp jaggery or sugar
a few curry leaves
1 cup oil, 1 tsp salt

Contd...

1. Mash tamarind. Strain to get tamarind water.
2. Heat 1 tbsp oil on a tawa. Add onions and roast the onions for 8-10 minutes till they soften and turn golden-brown. Keep aside.
3. On the same tawa dry-roast together - coriander seeds, sesame seeds, peanuts, cumin seeds, poppy seeds, kopra and the fenugreek seeds till they darken slightly and smell roasted.
4. Grind together the onions, roasted spices, ginger and garlic, salt, turmeric, red chilli powder and jaggery /sugar in a mixer into a fine paste. Add tamarind water to the mixer and again churn till smooth. Keep aside.
5. Heat oil in kadhai, and deep fry green chillies. As soon as the green chillies acquire a few golden-brown spots, remove from the pan and keep aside.
6. Heat 3-4 tbsp oil in a kadhai, add curry leaves to the oil and after a few seconds, add ground paste. Cook for about 5-10 minutes on medium flame.
7. Add the green chillies. Cook over medium heat, stirring occasionally. Add ½ cup water if the gravy appears too thick. Bring to a boil. Cook for another 4-5 minutes on slow flame till the oil comes to the surface.

Punjabi Matar Tamatar in Gravy

Peas with tomato chunks in a rich white gravy.

Serves 4

1 cup boiled or frozen peas
1 small firm tomato - cut into 4 pieces
3 tbsp oil
½ tsp jeera (cumin seeds)
2 onions and 1" piece ginger - ground to a paste together
2 tsp kasoori methi
1 tsp dhania powder
½ tsp garam masala
½ tsp red chilli powder
¼ tsp sugar
1 tsp salt or to taste
½ cup milk
1 tsp tandoori masala

GRIND TOGETHER TO A PASTE

2 tbsp kaju (cashewnuts) - soaked in ¼ cup hot water for 5 minutes
¾ cup dahi
seeds of 2 chhoti illaichi (green cardamoms)

1. Drain cashewnuts and grind along with curd and seeds of chhoti illaichi to a fine paste.
2. Heat 3 tbsp oil. Add jeera. Wait till it turns golden.
3. Add onion and ginger paste. Stir fry on low flame till light brown. Reduce flame.
4. Add kasoori methi, dhania powder, garam masala, red chilli, sugar and salt. Stir for ½ minute.
5. Gradually add curd-cashewnut mixture, a little at a time, stirring continuously. Bhuno for 4-5 minutes till masala turns thick and oil separates.
6. Add milk and 1 cup water. Boil. Simmer for 5-7 minutes, on low flame till gravy turns thick.
7. Add boiled peas. Mix.
8. Add tomato pieces and tandoori masala. Give 2-3 boils. Serve hot.

Yellow Curries

Scooping of mushrooms

Capsicums in Sesame Curry

Stir fried capsicum fingers in a til flavoured yellow gravy.

Picture on page 39   Serves 4

4 tbsp til (sesame seeds) - roasted on a tawa (griddle) till they start to change colour
2 tbsp desiccated coconut (coconut powder)
4 tbsp curd
4 capsicums - slice into thin fingers & remove seeds
1 tsp jeera (cumin seeds)
2 onions - finely chopped
2 tbsp tomato ketchup
4-5 fresh green chillies - chopped finely
1¼ tsp salt
½ tsp haldi
¼-½ tsp red chilli powder
½ tsp sugar
6 tbsp oil

1. Grind coconut and til in a grinder with 4 tbsp curd to a fine paste.
2. Heat 4 tbsp oil in a kadhai, add jeera. Wait till it gets golden.
3. Add onions and fry till golden brown in colour.
4. Add haldi, salt and chilli powder. Stir.
5. Add the coconut-til paste. Bhuno and cook till oil separates. Sprinkle some water in between if the paste sticks to the sides of the kadhai.
6. Add tomato ketchup and green chillies. Stir.
7. Add 1½ cups of water and sugar. Give 2-3 boils. Simmer for 3-4 minutes. Remove from fire.
8. Heat 2 tbsp oil in a pan or kadhai, add sliced capsicum and stir fry them for a few minutes or till they get brown patches and get slightly wilted or soft. Sprinkle ¼ tsp salt and mix. Keep aside till serving time.
9. At serving time, heat gravy and add fried capsicums. Mix well, cook for a minute. Serve hot.

Kandhari Bharwaan Khumb

*Red pomegranates and cheese stuffed in mushrooms and
put in a cardamom flavoured yellow gravy!*

Picture on page 1   *Serves 6-8*

200 gms mushrooms (12-15 big size pieces)
juice of ½ lemon, 2 tsp salt
1 cup red kandhari anaar ke daane (fresh red pomegranate)

FILLING
50 gms khoya - grated (½ cup)
1 small onion - chopped, ½" piece ginger-grated
1 tbsp kaju - crushed on a chakla belan
3 tbsp anaar ke daane .
3 tbsp chopped coriander
½ tsp garam masala
½ tsp black pepper
½ tsp bhuna jeera powder (roasted cumin)
2-3 big pinches of salt

GRAVY
3 onions
1½" piece ginger
4 dry red chillies
4 tbsp oil
4-5 chhoti illaichi (green cardamoms) - pounded to open slightly
½ tsp garam masala
½ tsp red chilli powder
½ tsp haldi
1 tsp dhania powder, 1½ tsp salt or to taste
1 cup milk
1 tbsp finely chopped coriander

1. Wash mushrooms and pull out the stalks. Hollow the mushrooms a little more with the help of a small scooper. (see the lower picture on page 45). Keep stalks aside.
2. Boil 4-5 cups water with 2 tsp salt and juice of ½ lemon. Add the mushrooms. Boil for 2 minutes. Drain and refresh with cold water. Strain. Wipe to dry well.

Contd...

3. For filling - heat oil in a kadhai, add onion, cook till soft. Add khoya, mix well. Add all the other ingredients given under filling. Mix well.
4. Stuff each mushroom with it. Place the mushrooms in a hot oven at 200°C for 3-4 minutes. Remove from oven and keep aside.
5. To prepare the gravy, blend the anaar ke daane with 1½ cups water in a mixer blender. Strain to get juice.
6. Trim the left over mushroom stalks. Grind mushroom stalks with onions, ginger and dry red chillies to a fine paste.
7. Heat 4 tbsp oil in a heavy kadhai. Add chhoti illaichi. Wait for a minute.
8. Add the onion-mushroom paste. Cook on low flame for about 7-8 minutes till onions turn light brown.
9. Add garam masala, red chilli powder, haldi, dhania and salt.
10. Add anaar ka ras. Boil, simmer for 5 minutes. Add milk to the gravy. Boil. Simmer on low flame for 5 minutes. Keep aside.
11. To serve, boil gravy. Pour in a serving dish. Arrange mushrooms on it. Heat in a microwave or an oven. Serve immediately, sprinkled with coriander & kaju.

Kate Baingan in Gravy

A curry flavoured with coconut. Serve it along with boiled rice for the main meal.

Serves 4-6

4 brinjals, about 400 gm (long, thin variety) - cut diagonally into 1" thick slices
2 onions - sliced
4 flakes garlic - finely chopped
2 tbsp curry powder (MDH) - mixed with 2 tbsp water
2¾ cups coconut milk fresh or readymade
2 tbsp curry leaves
3 tbsp oil
1 marbled sized ball of imli (tamarind) - soaked in ¼ cup water to get 2 tbsp of pulp
1 tsp salt, or to taste

1. Sprinkle ½ tsp salt on the brinjal slices. Mix well and keep aside for 20 minutes to sweat. Rinse in fresh water and wipe dry on a clean kitchen towel. Deep fry the brinjal slices till golden and keep aside till serving time.
2. Mash the soaked tamarind and take out the pulp.

3. Heat oil and fry onion slices and garlic until light golden.
4. Add curry powder paste and fry on low heat for 1 minute, until fragrant, making sure it does not burn.
5. Add coconut milk, 2 tbsp of tamarind pulp and curry leaves. Add salt to taste and bring to boil. Boil for 2-3 minutes on low heat.
6. To serve, add the fried brinjals to the gravy and boil for 2-3 minutes.
7. Serve hot with plain boiled rice.

Note : For fresh coconut milk, grate coconut and soak in 3 cups hot water for 10 minutes. Blend in a mixer and strain to get coconut milk.

Rajasthani Arbi

Chunks of arbi in a thin, delicious curd-besan gravy. Relish it with rice!

Serves 4-5

300 gm arbi (calocassia)
1 cup curd
2 tsp besan (gram flour)
1 tbsp ginger-garlic paste
¼ tsp haldi powder
1 tsp red chilli powder
1 tsp salt
3-4 laung (cloves), 2 moti illaichi (black cardmom)
1 tsp ajwain (carom seeds)
4 tbsp oil

1. Pressure cook arbi with 3 cups water to give 1 whistle and then keep on low heat for 3 minutes. Remove from fire. Peel arbi. Cut into ¾" thick slices.
2. Mix curd, besan, 1 cup water, ginger-garlic paste, salt, red chilli powder and haldi.
3. Heat oil in a kadhai, add laung, moti illaichi and ajwain. Let them splutter for a minute.
4. Add ¼ tsp salt and ½ tsp garam masala. Add arbi pieces and fry for 7-8 minutes till the stickiness is no more there and the arbi turns light brown.
5. Add the besan-curd mixture. Boil. Cook on low flame for about 3-4 minutes. Remove from fire. Garnish with coriander. Serve hot.

Achaari Paneer

Pickled flavoured masala paneer.

Serves 8   *Picture on page 2*

300 gms paneer - cut into 1½" cubes
2 capsicums - cut into 2" pieces
1" piece ginger & 5-6 flakes garlic - crushed to a paste
1 cup curd (dahi) - beat well till smooth
3 onions - chopped finely, 4 green chillies - chopped
½ tsp haldi (turmeric) powder, ¾ tsp garam masala
1 tsp amchoor (dried mango powder) or lemon juice to taste
2-3 green chillies - cut lengthwise into 4 pieces
1 tsp salt or to taste
½ cup milk mixed with ½ cup water
½ cup cream

ACHAARI MASALA

2 tsp saunf (aniseeds), 1 tsp rai (mustard seeds)
½ tsp kalonji (onion seeds)
a pinch of methi daana (fenugreek seeds), 1 tsp jeera (cumin seeds)

1. Cut paneer into 1½" cubes. Rub ½ tsp haldi, a pinch of salt and ½ tsp red chilli powder on the paneer and capsicum. Keep aside for 10 minutes.
2. Collect all seeds of the achaari masala - saunf, rai, kalonji, methi daana and jeera together in a plate.
3. Crush garlic and ginger roughly on a chakla-belan or use 2 tsp ginger-garlic paste.
4. Heat 4 tbsp oil. Add the collected seeds together to the hot oil. Let them crackle for 1 minute or till jeera turns golden.
5. Add onions and chopped green chillies. Cook till onions turn golden.
6. Add haldi and garlic-ginger paste. Cook for ½ minute.
7. Beat curd with ¼ cup water and a pinch of haldi till smooth. Add gradually and keep stirring. Add amchoor, garam masala and ¾ tsp salt (½ + ¼) or to taste. Cook for 2-3 minutes on low heat till the curd dries up a little. (Do not make it very dry). Remove from fire. Cool.
8. At serving time, add milk mixed with water and slit chillies. Boil on low heat for a minute, stirring continuously. Cook further for 2 minutes.
9. Add cream, paneer and capsicum, cook for a minute on low flame.

Rajasthani Bharwaan Lauki : Recipe on page 11 ➢

Paneer Makai Curry

Serves 4-6

100 gm paneer - cut into 1" cubes (8-10 pieces)
100 gm baby corns - slit into 2 pieces lengthways
4 tbsp oil
1 tej patta (bay leaf)
2-3 flakes garlic - crushed
1 large onion - ground to a paste
¾ tsp tandoori masala
¼ tsp sugar (optional)
a few capsicum rings or coriander leaves for garnishing

YOGURT PASTE
½ cup yogurt (curd)
2 tbsp cashewnuts (kaju) - soaked in warm water for 15 minutes
½ tsp haldi
1-2 green chillies
½ tsp salt, ½ tsp red chilli powder, ½ tsp garam masala

1. Soak kaju in warm water for 10 minutes. Drain and grind it along with all the ingredients of the yogurt - paste together to a smooth paste. Feel the paste with the fingers to check that the kajus are ground well.
2. Cut paneer into 1" cubes and deep fry the paneer to a golden colour.
3. For gravy, heat oil. Reduce heat. Add tej patta and garlic. Let garlic turn light brown.
4. Add onion and stir fry till golden.
5. Add the yogurt paste. Stir fry for 6-8 minutes on medium flame till dry and oil separates.
6. Add about 1 cup of water. Give one boil.
7. Add tandoori masala.
8. Add sugar, if the curry tastes sour (if the yogurt added is sour, sugar needs to be added).
9. Add babycorns. Cover and simmer curry for 5-6 minutes. Remove.
10. Add fried paneer to the gravy. Simmer for 3-4 minutes.
11. Transfer to a serving dish and garnish with 2-3 capsicum rings cut into halves or a few whole coriander leaves.

Shahi Kaju Aloo

Serves 6

300 gms (4) potatoes
4 tbsp cashews (kaju) - soaked in ½ cup water
1" piece ginger
4-5 flakes garlic
1 tsp shah jeera (black cumin)
1 tej patta (bay leaf)
2 onions - chopped
1 green chilli - deseeded and chopped
¼ tsp haldi (turmeric)
½ tsp garam masala
½ cup curd (yogurt) - whisked to make it smooth
2 tbsp chopped coriander
oil for frying and 4 tbsp oil

1. Wash potatoes and peel. Cut potatoes into 1" pieces.
2. Fry the potatoes to a deep golden brown on low medium heat and keep aside.
3. Grind cashews, ginger and garlic to a paste in a small coffee or spice grinder. Keep cashew paste aside.
4. Heat 4 tbsp oil in a heavy bottomed pan. Add shah jeera and tej patta. Wait for 30 seconds till jeera stops spluttering.
5. Add onions and green chilli. Cook on low heat till onions turn soft but do not let them turn brown. Add haldi and garam masala. Stir to mix well.
6. Add curd and stir fry till water evaporates. Cook till absolutely dry.
7. Add cashew paste and chopped coriander. Cook for 1-2 minutes.
8. Add about 1½ cups water to get a gravy. Boil and simmer uncovered on low heat for 5-7 minutes.
9. Add the fried potatoes to the gravy and simmer on low heat for 3-4 minutes. Serve hot.

Punjabi Kadhi

Gramflour dumplings in a tangy yoghurt curry.

Serves 4

¾ cup besan (gram flour)
2 cups sour curd (yoghurt)
½ tsp haldi powder, 2½ tsp salt or to taste
¾ tsp red chilli powder (according to taste)
2 tbsp oil
½ tsp jeera, ½ tsp methi daana (fenugreek seeds)
3-4 dry, red chillies, 4-5 curry leaves

PAKORAS (DUMPLINGS)
1 big onion - chopped finely, 1 big potato - chopped finely
½" piece ginger - chopped finely, 2 green chillies - chopped finely
½ tsp red chilli powder, 1 tsp salt, ½ tsp garam masala, 1 tsp dhania powder
a pinch of baking powder
1 cup besan, 1/3 cup water
oil for frying

TEMPERING/BAGHAR
1½ tbsp oil, ½ tsp jeera (cumin seeds), ¼ tsp red chilli powder

1. Mix curd, besan, salt, haldi, red chilli powder and 5½ cups water. Beat well till smooth and no lumps remain.
2. In a big heavy-bottomed pan, heat oil. Add jeera and methi seeds.
3. When jeera turns golden, add dry red chillies and curry leaves. Fry for 1 minute.
4. Add curd-water mixture. Stir continuously till it boils.
5. After one good boil, lower heat and simmer for 15 minutes, stirring in between. Keep aside.
6. To prepare pakoras, mix besan with water to make a paste. Beat well. Add all other ingredients given under pakoras. Beat well.
7. Heat oil and drop spoonfulls of batter. Deep fry pakoras till golden brown.
8. Add pakoras to the ready kadhi.
9. At serving time, transfer the hot kadhi to a serving dish.
10. To temper the kadhi, heat oil in small pan. Reduce flame and add jeera.
11. When it turns golden, remove from fire and add red chilli powder. Pour on to the hot kadhi in the dish. Serve with boiled rice.

Green Curries

Green Mushroom Curry

Serves 4

200 gms mushrooms

BATTER
¼ cup maida, 1½ tsp garlic paste
½ tsp each of salt, ½ tsp pepper, ¼-½ cup water approx.

PASTE-1
¼ cup freshly grated coconut
4 green chillies, 1 onion - roughly chopped, 3 flakes garlic
1 tbsp khus-khus (poppy seeds) - soaked in ¼ cup hot water for 10 minutes
3 tbsp badaam (almonds)
a blade of javetri (mace) - crushed to get ¼ tsp
seeds of 3 green chhoti illaichi (cardamoms), ½ tsp saunf (fennel seeds)

PASTE-2
1½ cups coriander leaves and stalks, 2 tbsp chopped poodina leaves (mint)

Contd...

OTHER INGREDIENTS
1 tsp jeera (cumin seeds), 1 tsp dhania powder (coriander powder)
1 tsp sugar, ½ tsp garam masala, ¼ tsp amchoor
¾ tsp salt, or to taste

1. Wash mushrooms well. Keep mushrooms whole and just trim the stalks, cutting only the end tip of the stem.
2. Mix all ingredients of the batter to make a smooth batter of coating consistency. Dip mushroom pieces in it and fry on low medium heat till light golden and cooked. Remove to a paper napkin and keep aside.
3. Grind all ingredients of paste-1 to a smooth paste along with the water.
4. Separately grind ingredients of paste-2 with ¼-½ cup water.
5. Heat 4 tbsp oil and add jeera. Let it turn golden. Add dhania powder.
6. Add the prepared paste- 1. Saute for 5-7 minutes, stirring continuously, adding a little water if the paste sticks to the sides of the kadhai.
7. Add the prepared paste - 2. Mix. Add sugar, salt, garam masala and amchoor. Cook for 3-4 minutes.
8. Add 2 cups of water. Give 2-3 boils. Simmer for 5 minutes.
9. At serving time, add the mushroom pieces & bring to a boil. Cook for 1-2 minutes over low heat. Remove from fire. Serve hot.

Broccoli Curry

An unusual preparation of broccoli florets in a tasty broccoli flavoured sauce.

Serves 5-6   *Picture on inside front cover*

1 medium flower of broccoli (hari gobhi)
1 large carrot - cut into ¼" thick slices, juice of ½ lemon
1 tbsp cashew halves (kaju tudka), 1 tsp raisins (kishmish)

CURRY

1 small flower (100 gm) of broccoli
2 onions - ground to a paste, 2 green chillies
1 tsp jeera (cumin seeds), ½ tsp ajwain (carom seeds)
1 tsp ginger-garlic paste
1½ tsp dhania powder, 1 tsp garam masala, a pinch of haldi
1 tsp salt or to taste, ½ tsp pepper or to taste
2 cups milk, 4 tbsp grated cheese (1½ Britannia cubes- grated)

1. Cut both flowers of broccoli into medium florets with some stalk.
2. Boil 5-6 cups water with 2 tsp salt, 1 tsp sugar and juice of ½ lemon. Add broccoli florets and carrots to boiling water. When a proper boils comes, remove from fire. Drain. Refresh in cold water. Strain. Pat dry.

3. Heat 1 tbsp butter and saute all the broccoli florets and carrots in it for 3-4 minutes. Sprinkle some salt and pepper.
4. Separate half of the broccoli and chop roughly into smaller pieces for the curry. Leave the remaining half florets whole.
5. Grind the roughly chopped broccoli and green chillies with 1 cup milk to a smooth green puree in a grinder.
6. For the gravy, heat 3 tbsp oil in a kadhai. Add kaju and kishmish. Stir till kaju turn golden. Remove from oil and keep aside.
7. To the hot oil, add 1 tsp jeera and ½ tsp ajwain. Let jeera turn golden.
8. Add onion paste. Cook on low heat till oil seperates. Do not let it turn brownish. Add ginger-garlic paste. Stir for a minute.
9. Add dhania powder, garam masala, haldi & salt to taste. Mix well.
10. Add pureed broccoli. Cook, stirring on low heat till oil separates.
11. Add 1 cup milk, stirring continuously. Stir till it boils. Cook for 2 minutes. Add ½ cup water to thin down the gravy. Do not make it too thin.
12. Add pepper to taste. Boil. Simmer for a minute. Add cheese. Remove from fire.
13. At the time of serving, heat gravy and add sauted broccoli and carrots along with nuts. Boil. Serve hot sprinkled with some grated cheese.

Paalak Chaman

Serves 4

250 gms paalak (spinach) - chopped (2½ cups)
a pinch of sugar
4 tbsp kasoori methi (dry fenugreek leaves)
200 gm paneer - cut into ¼" cubes and deep fried
2 tbsp cashewnuts (kaju) - soaked in warm water for 20 minutes and ground to a paste
½ stick dalchini (cinnamon)
2 chhoti illaichi (green cardamoms)
3-4 laung (cloves)
2 onions - ground to a paste
1/3 cup malai or cream
salt to taste, a pinch of sugar

BAGHAR/CHOWK (TEMPERING)
1 tbsp desi ghee, ½ tsp red chilli powder

1. Boil spinach in ½ cup water with a pinch of sugar. Cover and cook on low flame for 4-5 minutes till spinach turns soft. Remove from fire. Cool and blend to a puree.
2. Fry tiny pieces of paneer till golden brown.
3. Crush dalchini, laung & seeds of chhoti illaichi to a rough powder. Keep aside.
4. Grind kaju separately with a little water to a paste.
5. Heat 2 tbsp oil. Add onions and cook on low heat till oil separates and they turn light brown.
6. Add the freshly ground masala. Cook for a few seconds.
7. Add the kasoori methi and paalak. Bhuno for 5-7 minutes till dry.
8. Add malai or cream, cook on low heat for 3-4 minutes.
9. Add the fried paneer.
10. Add kaju paste and cook for a few seconds.
11. Add salt and sugar to taste. Simmer for a few minutes.
12. To serve, heat 1 tbsp desi ghee for the baghar. Remove from fire. Add red chilli powder to it and pour over paalak. Serve immediately.

Matar Dhania Wale

Peas with a green coriander paste.

Serves 4-5

2 cups shelled peas
2-3 tbsp oil
a pinch of hing (asafoetida)
1 tsp jeera (cumin seeds)
½ tsp kalonji (onion seeds)
1 tsp salt, or to taste
1 firm tomato - cut into 8 pieces and pulp removed
½ tsp garam masala
¾ cup water

DHANIA CHUTNEY
2 cups chopped coriander leaves
4 flakes garlic, 1½" piece of ginger
2 green chillies, 1 tomato

Contd...

CASHEW PASTE
2 tbsp kaju (cashewnuts) - grind to a paste with ¼ cup water

1. Grind together all the ingredients of the dhania chutney.
2. Heat 3 tbsp oil in the pressure cooker. Add hing, jeera and kalonji.
3. When jeera turns golden, add peas. Bhuno for 2-3 minutes.
4. Add dhania chutney to the peas and mix well. Add salt. Pressure cook to give 1 whistle. Open the cooker after the pressure drops.
5. Add cashew paste. Stir to mix well. Add enough water (¾ cup) to get a gravy. Boil. Simmer for a minute.
6. Add tomato and ½ tsp garam masala. Mix well. Serve hot.

Paneer in Pista Gravy

*A rich Mughlai style of cooking paneer with pista paste,
giving the curry a lovely green colour and flavour.*

Serves 6   *Picture on page 75*

300 gm paneer - cut into 1" squares
2 large onions
½ cup yogurt - beat well till smooth, 4 tbsp oil
1" ginger piece and 4-5 flakes garlic - crushed to a paste
1 tbsp dhania powder (ground coriander)
½ tsp white pepper powder, 1 tsp salt, or to taste
½ cup fresh cream
½ tsp garam masala powder

GRIND TOGETHER TO A PASTE WITH ¼ CUP WATER

½ cup pistas (pistachio nuts) with the hard cover - skinned, soaked and peeled
1 green chilli - finely chopped
¼ cup chopped fresh coriander

1. Peel and cut onions into 4 pieces. Boil in 1 cup water for 2-3 minutes. Drain, cool slightly and grind to a paste. Keep boiled onion paste aside.
2. Soak pistas in hot water for 10 minutes, drain and peel. Reserve a few peeled pistas for garnish.
3. Grind the remaining peeled pistas with chopped green chillies and coriander to a fine green paste with ¼ cup water.
4. Heat 4 tbsp oil in a kadhai, add boiled onion paste and saute for 7-8 minutes on low heat till dry and oil separates. See that the colour of the onions does not change to brown.
5. Add ginger-garlic paste and stir-fry for a minute.
6. Add coriander powder, white pepper powder and salt and mix well.
7. Stir in pista and green chilli paste. Cook for 2 minutes on low heat.
8. Add 1½ cups water and simmer on low heat for 2-3 minutes.
9. Add paneer. Mix.
10. Stir in curd and continue to simmer for 1 minute, stirring continuously.
11. Add cream, sprinkle garam masala powder and transfer to a serving dish. Sprinkle remaining pistas and some cream. Serve hot.

Paneer in Pista Gravy: Recipe on page 73 ➤

Chutney Wale Aloo

Whole potatoes simmered in a tangy mint flavoured gravy.

Serves 5-6

8 baby potatoes - keep whole or 3 potatoes - each cut into 2" pieces

HARI CHUTNEY

1 cup chopped fresh coriander, ½ small raw mango or ½ tsp amchoor
½ cup poodina (mint), ½ tsp salt, ½ tsp sugar

GRAVY

1 tsp jeera (cumin) seeds
2 onions - ground to a paste
4 tsp ginger -garlic paste
1 cup yoghurt and 2 tbsp kaju (cashewnuts) - ground to a paste till smooth
1 cup water, 4 tbsp oil
1 tsp salt, or to taste, 1 tsp red chilli powder
1 tomato - chopped finely
½ tsp garam masala

1. Peel and wash potatoes. Heat oil in a kadhai and deep fry over low heat until cooked and light brown in colour. Keep aside.
2. For the hari chutney, put all ingredients in a blender and make a paste. Keep chutney aside.
3. Grind kaju and yoghurt to a smooth paste.
4. Heat oil in a kadhai. Add jeera, wait for a minute till golden.
5. Add onion paste, stir over low heat until transparent. Do not brown the onions.
6. Add the ginger and garlic pastes and stir until the oil leaves the masala.
7. Add yoghurt and kaju paste. Stir for 1- 2 minutes.
8. Add hari chutney and red chilli powder. Stir till oil separates and the mixture turns dry.
9. Add 1 cup water, stirring continuously on low heat till it comes to a boil.
10. Now add the fried potatoes and salt. Simmer uncovered for 5 minutes until the oil leaves the masala and the gravy turns thick.
11. Add chopped tomato and garam masala, stir and bring to a boil. Serve.

Note: Do not cover the kadhai while cooking.

Malai Kofte in Paalak

Serves 6-8

KOFTAS (12-13)

100 gm paneer - mashed
2 slices bread - remove sides, 3 tbsp curd, 1/8 tsp baking powder
1 green chilli - chopped finely, 1 tbsp finely chopped coriander
½ tsp salt or to taste, ½ tsp pepper or to taste, ¼ tsp red chill powder
1½ tbsp maida (plain flour), a few pieces of kaju (cashewnuts)

GRAVY

1 tsp dhania powder, ½ tsp red chilli powder, ¼ tsp garam masala, salt to taste

BOIL TOGETHER

½ kg spinach leaves - chopped, 1 green chilli - chopped, 1" ginger - chopped

GRIND TOGETHER

2 onions, 2 tomatoes, 2 laung (cloves)

TADKA/TEMPERING

1 tbsp desi ghee, 1" ginger & 1 green chilli chopped, ½ tsp chilli powder

1. To prepare koftas, spread ¾ tbsp curd on each slice of bread to wet it. After spreading curd on both sides of bread, keep aside for a minute.
2. Mash the paneer well. Add baking powder, green chillies and coriander.
3. Mash the bread slices well and mix with the paneer. Add salt, pepper and red chilli powder to taste. Add maida in the end. Mix well.
4. Make balls and stuff a piece of cashew in the centre.
5. Deep fry 4-5 pieces at a time, in medium hot oil and keep aside.
6. For gravy, wash paalak and chop roughly. Boil palak with a green chilli and ginger. Cook covered for 3 minutes after it boils. Remove from fire.
7. Cool. After the spinach cools, blend to a paste and keep aside.
8. Grind onions, tomatoes and 2 laung to a paste.
9. Heat 4 tbsp oil. Add onion - tomato paste and cook stirring till dry.
10. Add dhania powder, chilli powder and salt to taste. Bhuno till oil separates.
11. Add the ground spinach and bhuno for 2-3 minutes. Add ½ cup water to make a thin green gravy and bhuno for 5 minutes. Add garam masala.
12. At serving time, heat the spinach gravy and add koftas. Stir gently on low flame for a minute. Remove from fire and transfer to a dish.
13. For tadka, heat ghee, add ginger. When it turns golden, shut off the flame. Add chillies and chilli powder, immediately pour over the koftas.

Hari Dal

A nutritive combination of dal and spinach.

Serves 6

½ cup channe ki dal (split gram), ½ kg paalak (spinach)
2 tomatoes, 1-2 green chillies - chopped, ½" piece ginger - chopped
1 tsp coriander powder, ½ tsp garam masala, ½ tsp red chilli powder
1 onion - chopped, 3 tbsp oil

CHOWK/TEMPERING

2 tbsp oil, ½ tsp rai, 1 small tomato- sliced and pulp removed

1. Soak dal for ½ hour. Wash, chop paalak leaves. Discard the stems.
2. Heat 3 tbsp oil in a pressure cooker. Fry onions till golden brown.
3. Strain the soaked dal. Add this dal, paalak and all other ingredients, including the spices and ¼ cup water.
4. Pressure cook to give 2 whistles, then cook on low heat for 8-10 minutes.
5. Remove from fire. After the pressure drops down, mash the dal slightly.
6. For tempering, heat oil, add rai, wait for few seconds. Add tomato and cook for a minute. Remove from fire. Pour on the dal.

2 cups coconut milk (ready-made, tetra pack) or 1 packet coconut milk powder (maggi)
mixed with 2 cups of water

BATTER
½ cup besan, 3 tbsp chopped coriander
½ tsp each of salt, garam masala & pepper

1. Grind coconut, whole chillies, jeera, saboot dhania, haldi, imli, ginger, garlic and ½ cup water to a paste. Keep coconut paste aside.
2. Heat 4-5 tbsp oil in a kadhai. Add the onions and saute till golden brown.
3. Add the tomatoes and cook for 5-6 minutes or till oil separates.
4. Add the ground coconut paste, cook on slow fire for 8-10 minutes.
5. Add coconut milk. Boil, stirring in between. Add salt to taste. Remove from fire.
6. Mix all the ingredients given under batter with about ¼ cup water to get a thick batter. Dip the paneer pieces in this batter and deep fry to a golden colour.
7. At the time of serving, add the fried paneer to the gravy and heat thoroughly. Serve hot.

Vegetable Sticks in Curry

Masala vegetables arranged on toothpicks & served with a spicy gravy.

Picture on facing page   *Serves 4*

1 big potato
5-6 french beans
2 carrots
few toothpicks

FOR DRY MASALA

2 tsp saboot dhania (coriander seeds), 1½ tsp jeera (cumin seeds)
1 tsp red chilli powder
½ tsp haldi (turmeric powder)
6-7 laung (cloves)
seeds of 6 moti illaichi (brown cardamom)
5-8 saboot kali mirch

GRIND TOGETHER

2 onions - roughly chopped
½" piece ginger - chopped

OTHER INGREDIENTS
3-4 tbsp oil
a pinch of hing (asafoetida)
2 tsp of the above masala
2 tomatoes - chopped
water - kept aside of the boiled vegetables
½ tsp shredded ginger
¼ tsp amchoor (dried mango powder)
½ tsp garam masala
salt to taste

1. Grind all ingredients of the dry masala together. Keep aside 2 tsp from this ground masala separately for the vegetables.
2. Peel potatoes & cut each into ½" pieces or squares. Deep fry to a golden colour.
3. Cut carrots into ¼" thick rounds. String french beans & cut into ½" long pieces.
4. Boil 2 cups of water with ½ tsp salt. Add beans and carrots. Boil for about 5 minutes or till tender. Strain, reserve the water for the gravy.
5. For curry, heat oil. Add hing. Add the ground dry masala.
6. Add the onion-ginger paste, cook till light brown and oil separates.

7. Add chopped tomatoes. Cook and mash till oil separates.
8. Add shredded ginger & sufficient water of boiled vegetables to get a thick gravy.
9. Add salt to taste, garam masala and amchoor. Simmer on low heat for 5-7 minutes.
10. Heat 2 tbsp oil seperately in a pan. Add the 2 tsp reserved ground masala.
11. Immediately add the fried potato, boiled beans and carrot and ¼ tsp salt. Mix well for 2 minutes, so that masala coats the vegetables.
12. On a toothpick, insert a potato piece, then french bean and lastly a piece of carrot.
13. Make many such toothpicks and keep aside in an oven proof dish.
14. At serving time heat the prepared toothpicks in a hot oven for 2-3 minutes or microwave for a minute. Pour hot gravy on top and serve immediately.

Mughlai Dum Aloo

Serves 4

5 (250 gm) small sized potatoes
3 onions - sliced finely
3 small tomatoes - chopped roughly
1" piece ginger - chopped
½ tsp jeera (cumin seeds)
½ tsp red chilli powder
½ tsp garam masala
¼ tsp amchoor
1¼ tsp salt or to taste
3 tbsp oil

SOAK TOGETHER FOR 10 MINUTES IN HOT WATER
3 tbsp magaz (watermelon seeds)
1 tbsp khus khus (poppy seeds)

1. Peel and cut potatoes into two equal halves. Deep fry on medium flame till golden brown. Remove from oil and keep aside. Check with a knife that the potatoes are cooked before removing from oil.
2. Deep fry sliced onions to a golden brown colour. Remove from oil and grind the fried onions to a paste with a little water if required. Keep fried onion paste aside.
3. Soak magaz and khus khus together in ¼ cup hot water for 10 minutes. Grind to a fine paste.
4. Boil tomatoes, ginger and ½ cup water together in a pan. Cover and cook till water dries up and the tomatoes turn soft. Grind to a paste.
5. Heat 3 tbsp oil. Add jeera. When it splutters, add red chilli powder.
6. Add the fried onion paste. Cook for 2 minutes on low flame.
7. Add the tomato paste. Cook for 4-5 minutes on low flame till oil separates.
8. Add magaz-khus khus paste, salt, garam masala and amchoor. Stir for 2 minutes.
9. Add 1 cup water. Boil. Add fried potatoes. Simmer on low heat for 5-7 minutes till potatoes are well cooked and coated with masala.
10. Serve hot garnished with chopped coriander and magaz.

Nawabi Guchhi

Serves 4

100 gms (½ packet) mushrooms - cut into halves
1 cup shelled peas
3 tbsp ghee
2 tbsp coriander leaves - chopped
½ tsp garam masala, ½ tsp red chilli powder
¾ tsp salt, or to taste

NAWABI PASTE

2 onions
1" piece ginger
¼ cup kaju (cashewnuts)
½ tsp shahi jeera (black cumin)
½ tsp ordinary jeera (cumin seeds)
1 green chilli
1 dry, red chilli

1. Grind the onions and the cashewnuts along with all the other ingredients of the nawabi paste with a little water to a paste.
2. Heat the ghee and fry the nut and onion paste to a rich golden colour, sprinkling a little water now and then to prevent it from burning. Fry till ghee separates.
3. Add the garam masala and chilli powder. Stir for a few seconds.
4. Add ½ cup water. Boil. Add the mushrooms and peas. Bhuno for 4-5 minutes on low flame.
5. Add 1 cup of water and 1 tbsp coriander leaves. Cook covered on low flame, till the vegetables are done.
6. Remove from fire when the vegetables are cooked & the gravy is slightly thick.
7. Serve hot, garnished with fresh coriander leaves.

Paneer Chettinad

The fiery, delicious, brown curry of Chettinad - a place in South India.

Serves 4-6

250 gm paneer - cut into 1½" pieces and fried till golden
4 tbsp oil
1 large onion - finely chopped
10-12 curry patta
3 tomatoes - chopped
½ tsp haldi, 1 tsp chilli powder, 1½ tsp salt, or to taste
1 tbsp lemon juice or to taste
1" piece ginger, 8-10 flakes garlic
1 tbsp khus khus (poppy seeds) and 2 tbsp cashewnuts - soak together in hot water

CHETTINAD MASALA (ROASTED AND GROUND)
½ cup freshly grated coconut (remove brown skin before grating)
1 tsp saboot dhania (coriander seeds), ½ tsp jeera (cumin seeds)
1 tsp saunf (fennel), 2-3 dry, whole red chillies
seeds of 3 chhoti illaichi (green cardamoms), 2-3 laung (cloves)
1" dalchini (cinnamon stick), 1 tbsp oil

1. Soak khus khus and cashewnuts in a little warm water for 10-15 minutes.
2. For the chettinad masala, heat 1 tbsp oil in a kadhai or tawa. Add coconut, saboot dhania, jeera, saunf, red chillies, laung, dalchini and seeds of chhoti illaichi to oil. Stir-fry for 3-4 minutes till fragrant and golden. Remove from fire.
3. Drain khus and cashews. Grind together the roasted masala with the drained khus-khus-cashewnuts, ginger and garlic in a mixer blender to a very smooth paste using about ½ cup water.
4. Heat oil in a kadhai and add the chopped onions. Fry till golden.
5. Add the ground paste and curry leaves. Saute for ½ a minute.
6. Add the chopped tomatoes, salt, haldi and chilli powder. Cook for about 10 minutes on medium flame till tomatoes are well blended.
7. Add lemon juice and 1½ cups of water. Boil. Simmer for 5-7 minutes. If you desire a thinner gravy, add some more water and give 3 quick boils.
8. Add paneer and boil. Simmer for 4-5 minutes. Garnish with coriander.

Parval ka Dum

Aloo and parval in a thick gravy flavoured with whole spices.

Serves 4

250 gm parval
5 baby potatoes or 1 regular potato - cut into 8 pieces
2 large onions - finely sliced lengthwise
2 tsp ginger-garlic paste
2 tomatoes - finely chopped
2 tbsp ghee, 2 tbsp oil
½ tsp jeera (cumin seeds)
1 tej patta (bay leaves)
2 cloves (laung), 2-3 sticks dalchini (cinnamon)
2-3 moti illaichi (black cardamoms)
1 tbsp dhania powder, ½ tsp garam masala, 1¼ tsp salt, or to taste
½ cup curd - beat well till smooth
1 tbsp tomato puree
a pinch of javetri (mace) powder (crush a tiny blade of javetri)

1. Scrape the parval to lightly remove the peel. Cut it into half lengthwise and cut each piece into two to get fingers. Wash and peel the potatoes.
2. Heat oil and ghee together in a pressure pan, add jeera. Let it turn golden. Add the parvals and stir fry till the skin changes colour. Remove from oil. Saute the potatoes in oil for 2 minutes and keep aside.
3. In the left over oil, about ¾ tbsp oil, add more oil to make it to 2 tbsp. Heat oil and add all the whole garam masalas - tej patta, laung, dalchini and moti illaichi. Wait for a minute.
4. Add onion and cook on low flame till it turns brown. Add dhania powder, garam masala and salt.
5. Add the ginger-garlic paste and fry for 2-3 minutes.
6. Add the tomatoes and keep stirring till they turn very soft.
7. Add the curd and bhuno on low heat, stirring for 5 minutes. Add the tomato puree also. Cook till oil separates.
8. Add the potatoes and parvals and mix well. Add 1 cup water. Add mace powder. Cover the cooker and pressure cook till one whistle.
9. When cool, open the lid and see if the consistency is right.
10. Garnish with green coriander. Serve hot.

Dal Makhani

Picture on page 103   *Serves 6*

1 cup urad saboot (whole black beans)
1 tbsp ghee or oil
1½ tsp salt
3 tbsp ghee or oil
5 tomatoes - pureed in a grinder
2 tsp dhania powder (coriander)
½ tsp garam masala
1 tbsp kasoori methi (dry fenugreek leaves)
2 tsp tomato ketchup
2-3 tbsp butter
½ cup milk
½ cup cream
a pinch of jaiphal (nutmeg) - grated

GRIND TO A PASTE
2 dry, whole red chillies, preferably Kashmiri red chillies - deseeded & soaked for
10 minutes and then drained
1" piece ginger
5-6 flakes garlic

1. Pressure cook dal with 5 cups water, 1 tbsp ghee, salt and half of the ginger-garlic-chilli paste.
2. After the first whistle, keep on low flame for 40 minutes. Remove from fire. After the pressure drops, mash the hot dal a little. Keep aside.
3. Heat ghee. Add tomatoes pureed in a grinder. Cook until thick and dry.
4. Add the garam masala and coriander powder. Cook until ghee separates.
5. Add kasoori methi and the left over ginger-garlic-chilli paste. Cook further for 1-2 minutes.
6. Add this tomato mixture to the boiled dal. Add tomato ketchup also.
7. Add butter. Simmer on low flame for 15-20 minutes, stirring and mashing the dal occasionally with a karchhi against the sides of the cooker.

Contd...

8. Add milk. Mix very well with a karchhi. Simmer for 10 minutes more, to get the right colour and smoothness.
9. Reduce heat. Add jaiphal. Mix. Add cream gradually, stirring continuously. Remove from fire. Serve.

Note: Originally the dal was cooked by leaving it overnight on the burning coal angithis. The longer the dal simmered, the better it tasted.

Indian
Rice & Breads
Paranthas, Nans & Rotis

Onion & Mint Rice

Serves 4

3 cups boiled rice
3 onions - sliced very finely
3/4 cup mint (poodina) leaves - finely chopped, washed well and drained
3 tbsp oil
1 tsp salt or to taste
½ tsp garam masala, a pinch of haldi, ½ tsp red chilli powder

1. Heat oil in a non stick wok or kadhai. Add onion slices and stir fry till well browned & crisp. Do not burn them but make them dark brown. Reduce flame.
2. Add 1 tbsp water. Add garam masala, a pinch of haldi and chilli powder.
3. Add the poodina leaves. Mix.
4. Fluff boiled rice with a fork. Add to the onions. Mix well. Sprinkle salt and stir fry for 2-3 minutes. Serve with any curry or dal.

Lachha Parantha

Makes 6

2 cups atta (wheat flour), ½ tsp salt, 2 tbsp ghee, ½ cup milk, ½ cup water

1. Sift flour and salt in a paraat. Mix in 1 tbsp ghee till the flour turns crumbly.
2. Mix water and milk together. Make a well in the middle of the flour. Pour milk-water mix gradually. Knead well to a dough of rolling consistency. Keep covered with a damp cloth for ½ hour.
3. Make 6 balls. Roll out each ball to a circle of 6" diameter. Spread some ghee all over. Sprinkle dry atta on half of the circle.
4. Fold into ½ to get semi-circle. Spread ghee all over again. Put dry atta on ½ of semi-circle. Fold again lengthwise into ½. You get a long strip.
5. Apply ghee all over on the strip. Roll the strip from one end till the end, to form a flattened ball (pedha). Press gently. Roll out, applying very little pressure, to form the lachha parantha. If too much pressure is applied, the layers stick to each other and do not open up later.
6. Stick in a heated tandoor or shallow fry on a tawa. Place on a clean napkin and crush the parantha slightly, to open up the layers.

Tandoori Roti

Makes 6-7

2½ cups atta (whole wheat flour), ½ tsp salt, 1 cup water (approx.)

PASTE TO SPREAD
2 tbsp ghee or oil mixed with 1 tbsp maida

1. Make a soft dough with atta, salt and water. Keep aside for half an hour.
2. Divide the dough into 6 equal balls. Flatten each ball, roll out each into a round of 5" diameter.
3. Spread some ghee mixed with maida.
4. Make a slit, starting from any one end till almost to the other end, leaving just 1".
5. Start rolling from the slit, to form an even cone.
6. Keeping the cone upright, press slightly to get a flattened, coiled disc.
7. Roll out with a belan to a diameter of 5", applying pressure only at the centre and not on the sides. The layers do not open if pressure is applied on the sides. Cook in a hot tandoor till brown specs appear.

Vegetable Korma: Recipe on page 34, Dal Makhani: Recipe on page 96 ➤

BEST SELLERS BY  SNAB
Excellence in Books

Biryanis & Pulaos

Baking Recipes

Baby Cookbook

Microwave Cakes & Snacks

Diet Snacks & Desserts

Microwave Recipes - Vegetarian

Indian Favourites Vegetarian

Lebanese Recipes

Pasta Recipes Vegetarian

Sandwiches & Wraps

Paranthas & Rice for Kids

Recipes for Growing Kids